FIRST THINGS FIRST

Practical Steps to Victorious Living

Deborah Y. Evans

"FIRST THINGS FIRST"
Copyright @ 2004 by Deborah Y. Evans

ISBN: 1-59352-107-3

Printed in the United States of America.

Publishing

Christian Services Network
1975 Janich Ranch Ct.
El Cajon, CA 92019
1-866-464-6184
www.csnbooks.com

Additional copies of this book are available at local bookstores and through Victorious Living Now Ministries.

www.victoriouslivingnow.org

TABLE OF CONTENTS

DEDICATION

Thank You Heavenly Father for reminding me of the first things in my relationship with You. I give You praise and honor for using my life for Your glory!

I dedicate this first fruit to a wonderful man, faithful supporter, encourager and best friend, my husband, Roger. Thanks for always encouraging me to "Go for it." The best is yet to come.

. . .   to our princess and prince, Gabrielle and Raphael. Thanks for your love, support and prayers for mom to do her best.

. . .   to the best Pastor and "Champion," Timothy L. Seay, for believing in me and encouraging me to excel and take risks.

. . .   to the many who assisted in the delivery process and came alongside as spiritual midwives in support, prayer and encouragement to fulfill what God has begun in me. Thank you all!

First Things First

Practical Steps to Victorious Living

FOREWORD

"I have had the pleasure of knowing Pastor Deborah Evans for over 25 years, from the infancy of her walk with the Lord, to the maturity of her flowing with Pastoral authority. Over the years, she has been marked by consistency, integrity, and a pure pursuit for the purpose of God. I strongly encourage you to receive this vessel in which there is present an anointing that is able to take you to new places in your relationship and purpose in God."

Pastor Timothy L. Seay
Emmanuel Covenant Church
Sr. Pastor & Founder

"Pastor Deborah Evans of Victorious Living Now Ministries is an anointed and dynamic teacher of the Word of God. Her heart for women is evidenced as she teaches and instructs women from all walks of life. Pastor Deborah is a treasure in the Body of Christ and an example for women everywhere."

Pastor Kitt Brewington
Victory Christian Church International
Gaithersburg, MD

"Pastor Deborah Evans is an anointed teacher of the word of God. Her ministry has been a tremendous blessing to Pastor Bridget and I, and the entire Love Foundation International Ministry."

Daniel Erhabor, Senior Pastor
Love Foundation International
Laurel, MD

"Pastor Deborah Evans is a profound speaker who takes the hidden things of God and delineates it to the listening audience with simplicity and theological accuracy. She is seasoned, equipped, and enveloped with the burden removing and yoke destroying power of God. Her ministry is one of excellence and, at this season, is being propelled forward and armed by the Holy Spirit to pierce the souls of mankind with God's revelation and purpose."

Bishop Avaneda D. Hobbs
Pastor, Sword of the Spirit International Ministries
Dumfries, VA

INTRODUCTION

*But Seek First the Kingdom and His Righteous-
ness; And All These Things Will Seek You Out.*
                                        (Matthew 6:31-33)

—J.B. Phillips

To seek is to search for, strive after, to make haste, to pursue consistently, to desire. *First Things First* is a call to wholeheartedly pursue and follow after God and His ways. Sometimes on this journey we lose our way, we make a wrong turn in the things we seek and pursue, losing sight of the standard of the kingdom.

No building can survive or weather the storms without a proper foundation. In our pursuit to get to another level in our relationship with Christ, or grow deeper, we must remember the key to our strength results in the depth of our roots. It's not deeper truths that we need, as much as, a return to pursuit of the kingdom and the appropriation of its reign in our lives.

Jesus often reminds us throughout scripture of the "first things" that are necessary in our pursuit of Him.

*Therefore if you bring your gift to the altar, and
there remember that your brother has something
against you, leave your gift there before the altar,
and go your way. First be reconciled to your
brother and then come and offer your gift.*
                                        (Matthew 5:23-24)

Yet we find ourselves overlooking or even trying to skip the *"first things."*

So often we attempt to get from one place to another without a road map. We automatically assume that because we know where we want to go, it's just a matter of putting the car in drive and hitting the accelerator. However, without the assistance of directions and basic essentials, we will make a lot of wrong turns, waste a lot of gas, time and energy. All of which will take us further away from our destination or desired goal.

We've all heard expressions, before you learn to walk, you must *first* learn to crawl; before you build a house, you must *first* lay the foundation; or, what about this one, you can't put the cart before the horse. Often in our pursuit to live for Christ, it's easy to stumble over the basic, elementary essentials unless we consider a few "first things" to assist us in reaching our destination successfully. Unfortunately, many are looking for the express route or what is commonly known as a short-cut in life. "Just tell me the fastest way to get what I want, or the quickest way to get where I want to go." Even in our relationship with God, we want the express route to blessings, victory, spiritual maturity and even financial prosperity.

To live for Christ requires adjusting our focus, not to simply look for the shortcuts. To live for Christ begins with "first" seeking the Kingdom, and the priorities of the Kingdom.

In Galatians 2:20, we are reminded,

I have been crucified with Christ; it is no longer I who live, but Christ lives in me; and the life which I now live in the flesh I live by faith in the Son of God who loved me and gave Himself for me.

Maybe you find yourself preoccupied or distracted by many things. It could be you desire a more fulfilling relationship with the One who gave Himself for you and want to start a fresh commitment with Him. Maybe you have come to the end of your shortcuts and realize to live for Christ is to live life on His terms, going back to the *first things*. Wherever you find yourself, I invite you to push the pause button, and re-focus your priorities as you discover *"First Things First, Practical Steps to Victorious Living."*

As we submit to the rule of Christ, we have full assurance that in *first* seeking Him, we won't need to seek *"other things,"* but *"all other things"* will seek us out! Wherever you are, hit the brakes, get off the expressway, and let's go back to the starting line. Grab a pen and get ready to make a fresh commitment to the *first things* that please the heart of God! Let's go.

Nevertheless I have this against you, that you have left your first love.

(Revelation 2:4)

CHAPTER ONE

First Seek To Be True Worshipers Of God

First-Things-First. Not everyone who calls themselves worshipers of God really worships God. Worship is revealed in that which occupies most of our time. We could be worshipers of our television, our cars, our telephones, or even other people. So often we become busy in the work of the Lord while neglecting the importance of that first love relationship that once captivated our hearts. Remember that moment where your heart longed to be in His presence, where your skin felt all tingly just because you knew He was present and you couldn't wait to tell someone about your experience and time spent with Him?

In Revelations 2, God calls the church of Ephesus back to what matters most, worship and loving Him. After mentioning all the works, labor, and zeal they had accomplished for His name's sake, He reminds them,

"Nevertheless I have this against you, that you have left your first love." Remember, therefore from where you have fallen; repent and do the first works.

These words echo God's heart for every child of His today. It is a call to examine our lives to discover what things, we too, have allowed to take us from our first love. It is so easy to allow other things or other people to gradually cause us to abandon the priority of Him who we need most. Living for Christ requires realigning our focus from the objects of self-worship, other worship or circumstantial worship to first worshiping the true and living God at all times; above all things " . . . *for the Father is seeking such to worship Him."* John 4:23 The "such" He is speaking of are the "true worshipers."

Somehow we feel that we can impress God with our works. However, as much as God is delighted to see His children serve Him with gladness, He takes pleasure in knowing that before we strive to be noticed for how great a job we've done or for all the mighty acts accomplished in His name, that our longing for Him would first exceed all other things.

As the deer pants for the water brooks, So pants my soul for You, O God.

(Psalm 42:1)

When we lose our thirst for God, we also lose our desire to worship God. *First Things First* requires living a life of worship. Worship: *"proskuneo,"* to kiss fervently, also means to prostrate oneself, bow down, show reverence and adoration for. Worship says, "I love you because of who you are, not because of what you do." A worshiper, who truly worships God, longs for moments to linger at the feet of their Beloved, just to be close, just to be near the One who alone is able to change, heal, and set us free. A worshiper responds to God's call to offer all other objects of affection in exchange for God's best. True worship always responds in surrender and obedience to God.

Anytime we lose sight of our priority to first be worshipers of God, we find ourselves becoming worshipers of other things and other persons, thus they become first in our life. It has been stated that whatever we worship we become, therefore, if our focus and adoration is more on ourselves and our problems, we become more selfish; if our focus and adoration is more for our works and busyness in the kingdom, we become religious. However, if our focus and adoration is toward God, we become more like Him, and, consequently, we can be His witnesses in the earth.

Whose image are you bearing lately? Are you bearing the image of your Heavenly Father? It is a true worshiper that acknowledges God is worthy of adoration, worthy of surrender, worthy of obedience...not when I feel like it or when I have a tangible blessing to show others, but rather, He is worthy because all that we are, all that we claim to know, all that we have is because of Him! We have life because of who He is, we exist because of and for Him. Is your highest priority to demonstrate unashamed adoration to the one who first loved you? To the one who pursued you relentlessly when no one else would listen or pay any attention to you?

When is the last time you simply spent an untimed, not watching the clock, not because your pastor asked you to, amount of time enjoying the presence of the Lord? Before you take another step, schedule another meeting, or give your attention or affections towards another, *First Things First*, reacquaint yourself with first being a worshiper of God, then all other things in your life will flow from an undistracted devotion of a first love relationship with your heavenly Father. The Father is still looking for those who will worship Him in Spirit and Truth. *First Things First, seek to be a true Worshiper of God!*

Nevertheless I have this against you, that you have left your first love.

(Revelation 2:4)

Do you long for God, or are you constantly longing for the affection of others to bring you satisfaction? Is it His face you long to seek? Have you become a worshiper of other things? In what ways do you need to renew your commitment to your "first love"?

_____

_____

_____

_____

_____

_____

_____

_____

_____

_____

_____

_____

_____

_____

_____

_____

_____

_____

_____

Closing prayer:

Heavenly Father, I make a new commitment today to put no other gods before You (not my desires, other people, my family, my career). I desire to seek Your face and to seek it with all my heart. Thank You, Lord, for reminding me to keep You at the center of all I do. Fan again the flames of my love for You!

Though I speak with the tongues of men and of angles, but have not love, I have become sounding brass or a clanging cymbal. And though I have the gift of prophecy, and understand all mysteries and all knowledge, and though I have all faith, so that I could remove mountains, but have not love, I am nothing. And though I bestow all my goods to feed the poor, and though I give my body to be burned, but have not love, it profits me nothing.

(1 Corinthians 13:1-4)

CHAPTER TWO

First Seek To Walk In Love

First Things First. How can we love God, whom we have never seen and hate our brother **[whom we see everyday]**? Everyone is looking for love or to be loved. "Somebody, anybody, just love me," are the cries of many in our society. Unfortunately, this has become the cry of many in the church, as well. "Somebody to love me." It is in this sought-after quest for love that many allow the walls of indifference to build, as they justify their inability to love due to the lack of being loved. I am reminded of these familiar words *"For God so loved the world that He gave His only begotten Son"* John 3:16. It is in these words that we discover our example of genuine love, as we see love is first given before it is ever received. God demonstrated His love toward us while we were still sinners. Imagine that, God loved us not because we were so great, or we were just thrilled to shower Him with love. Rather, when the thoughts of God and His standards were far from our hearts and mind, when we were drunk in our own self-sufficiency, when we dared to even speak of Him or acknowledge Him, He gave to us, He loved us. Yet, in spite of this great love towards us, we continue to gather in His name, speaking words of adoration to God, whom we cannot see, yet not practice love for our brother or sister standing right next to us in the worship service — whom we can see. How can we love God and not walk in love toward one another?

If someone says, 'I love God,' and hates his brother, he is a liar; for he who does not love his brother whom he has seen, how can he love God whom he has not seen?

(1 John 4:20)

First Things First. Before we can see answers to our prayers or the mighty workings of God's power flowing through us and in His Church, there must first be a willingness to walk in the love of God. Many believers spend the majority of their walk talking about love, but never yielding themselves as instruments through which God's love can flow. The love of God, fondly known as *"Agapao"* (to love), is a love that is not based on what is received or how it feels. It's not the *"I love you - you love me"* kind of love. It's not even the *"goose-bumps, butterflies-in-the-stomach"* love. Do you think God decided to give His only begotten Son because He had butterflies or goose bumps? Although I do believe we can and should feel love, our decision to walk in love must never be based on our feeling love. This love that God calls us to first walk in is not a love that says, what's in it for me? — rather, it is a love that asks what can I give? It's a sacrificial love that demonstrates itself not simply because of, but in spite of.

Love is an action word that has been reduced to a repetitious saying void of manifestation. Many believers seek to avoid the repetition of the words *"I love you"* for fear they are saying something they don't mean or feel. Both ideas separate us from our Christian calling – to love. For the child of God, love is not an option. Our profession as Christians has drafted us to represent Christ, thus, by nature of our new life, we are to be lovers. How can such an impossible task at times be a part of our Christian experience? God has graced us with the ability and power through Himself to love. He has poured His love into our hearts.

> *Now hope does not disappoint, because the love of God has been poured out in our hearts by the Holy Spirit who was given to us.*
>
> (Romans 5:8)

Therefore, what appears or seems to be impossible, becomes possible with God. When we recognize our complete dependency upon Him, we will discover the ability, in Christ, to love those who persecute or speak evil against, use, hurt, or forsake us and truly mean it! As believers, we are to demonstrate the Christ-like, unselfish, loyal, benevolent concern for the well-being of another.

First Things First, we must walk in love. It is through our demonstration of love toward one another that the manifestation of who God is becomes evident. The world is filled with rejection, betrayal, and hatred. When we, the body of Christ, can exhibit His love, others will see, the Kingdom of God has come and the manifestation and power of that Kingdom will be seen in our love.

> *A new commandment I give to you, that you love one another; as I have loved you, that you also love one another. By this all will know that you are My disciples, if you have love for one another.*
>
> (John 13:34-35)

Jesus wasn't suggesting to love one another based on how we are being loved. He calls us as His children, heirs of His Kingdom, to love one another as He has loved us. Ponder for a moment, how has He loved you? When you missed days, weeks and months without speaking to Him . . . He loved you. When He answered that long-awaited prayer request and you didn't even thank Him . . . He loved you. When He delivered you out of that *"thing"* you said, "I'll never do again," and a week later did it . . . He loved you. When He blessed you with the new job, increased salary, and you robbed Him by stealing the tithe . . . He loved you. When you stood in His presence and said, "Lord, I love you, it's You I desire," and you started spending more time with others than Him . . .He loved you. The next time you're tempted to feel justified not to walk in love and you tell yourself that another person doesn't deserve to be loved, remember how Jesus loved and continues to love you, and do likewise. Allow His love through the power of the Holy Spirit to empower you to love, that the world will know that we are His disciples. The absence of love is the absence of a genuine relationship with God.

Take a few moments and take the love test.

Love . . .

> is longsuffering
> is kind
> is not jealous
> is not boastful
> is not arrogant
> is not rude
> is not selfish
> is not resentful
> does not think evil
> rejoices in truth

bears all things
believes all things
hopes all things
endures all things
never fails.

How's your love walk?

(I Corinthians 13:1-13)

Though I speak with the tongues of men and of angels, but have not love, I have become sounding brass or a clanging cymbal. And though I have the gift of prophecy, and understand all mysteries and all knowledge, and though I have all faith, so that I could remove mountains, but have not love, I am nothing. And though I bestow all my goods to feed the poor, and though I give my body to be burned, but have not love, it profits me nothing.

(I Corinthians 13:1-4)

How is your love walk? Are you struggling to love and get along with someone God has placed in your life? Would you rather say nothing than to speak to them at all? Renew your commitment to walk in love.

_____

_____

_____

_____

_____

_____

_____

_____

_____

_____

_____

_____

_____

_____

_____

_____

Closing prayer:

Lord, it's not always easy to love, especially those who are closest to me. I lay aside the attitudes of the flesh (impatience, selfishness...) that hinder the manifestation of Your power to love through me. I choose to love. Thank You for reminding me love is not a feeling, and thank You for loving me! Amen.

The earth is the Lord's, and all its fullness, the world and those who dwell therein.

(Psalm 24:1)

CHAPTER THREE

First Seek to Honor God With Our Wealth

First Things First. Did you know that all you have belongs to the Lord? Yes, your family, your possessions, and even your money.

Will a man rob God? Yet you have robbed Me! But you say, In what way have we robbed You? In tithes and offerings.

(Malachi 3:8)

Before you are tempted to skip this chapter, *First Things First* requires first honoring God with what He has blessed us with. We don't mind hearing about 12 steps to financial freedom or 3 steps to receive a wealth transfer. However, stumbling over the decision to trust God and honor God with our wealth hinders us in receiving the blessings God so desires to release into our life. Before we seek the blessings, we must first make sure we are not in the category of those the Bible calls thieves.

In order for God to usher those blessings into our lives we must first acknowledge His ownership of all that we have, including our money. The psalmist declares in Psalm 24: 1, *"The earth is the Lord's, and all its fullness, the world and those who dwell therein."* Now pause for a moment and think, if the earth belongs to the Lord and the fullness of all that's in the earth, then that includes you and me and all that we have since we live on the earth. In this chapter, honoring God with our wealth refers to our attitude toward the tithe and offering. The word "honor" means to show respect or allegiance to.

A son honors his father, And a servant his master. If then I am the Father, Where is My honor? And if I am a Master, Where is My reverence? Says the Lord of Hosts.

(Malachi 1:6)

God was not being honored. Instead, He was being offered the defiled, blind, lame and the sick as an offering. What they failed to realize was that their offerings revealed their reverence or lack thereof toward God. When we decide that we will not tithe or bring an offering to God's house, it reflects our inner response toward the God we declare we love and trust. No matter how much we jump, shout and sweat out our clothes during worship, our attitude toward money, the tithe and offering reveal a heart of trust or a lack of trust in God.

First Things First, God is calling us to trust Him with all that we are and possess.

Bring all the tithes into the storehouse, That there may be food in My house, And try Me now in this," says the Lord of hosts, "If I will not open for you the windows of heaven and pour out for you such blessing that there will not be room enough to receive it.

(Malachi 3:7)

The word tithe means tenth. Tithing is the regular practice of setting aside the first tenth of all increase to God. To tithe is to give 10 percent of your gross income to the storehouse or the local church where you are a member. No matter how gross it may be to you, it belongs to the Lord. In this verse, God reveals four important points about the tithe: First, *"Bring all the tithes."* God can count. In other words, don't try to put a couple of dollars in the offering plate and call it a tithe. All means all, 10 percent of your gross income, 10 percent of your bonuses, or any monetary gifts received. Second, He tells us where to bring it, *"into the storehouse,"* which represented the temple or a local synagogue. A storehouse is where you find food, we receive spiritual food from our local church, which represents our storehouse. Third, He tells us the purpose of the tithe. *"So there would be food in His house."* Now, why is it important for God to have food in His house? I hope it didn't take you too long to answer that question...people like to eat. Everyone likes good food and in our churches, it's no different. We all like to hear a good sermon, a word from the Lord...something to sink our spiritual teeth in and chew on all week. In addition, we like for the places where we eat our food to be comfortable, clean, not too hot, not too cold. The tithe assists the church in advancing the Kingdom of God, preaching the gospel, and changing lives. Fourth, He assures us we can trust Him to take care of us.

Try Me now in this, says the Lord of hosts, if I will not open for you the windows of heaven and pour out for you such blessing that there will not be room enough to receive it.

There has often been much dispute over whether tithing is a biblical discipline to be practiced today. Some suggest that tithing is legalistic, being a part of the law, and thus not applicable. However, we see an account of the first tither in Genesis 14 when Abraham, our Father of Faith, gives a tithe to Melchizedek. Thus, tithing was practiced before the institution of the law.

In Genesis 14:17:

And the king of Sodom went out to meet him at the Valley of Shaveh.

(That is, the King's Valley), after his return from the defeat of Chedorlaomer and the kings who were with him. Then Melchizedek, King of Salem, brought out bread and wine; he was priest of God Most High. And he blessed him and said:

Blessed be Abram of God Most High, Possessor of heaven and earth; And blessed be God Most High, Who has delivered your enemies into your hand. And he gave him a tithe of all.

Abraham voluntarily gave a tenth of the spoils and recognized God as His source and the reason for his victory in the battle. Melchizedek is a foreshadow, a picture or type of Jesus. Melchizedek's name means "My King is Righteousness." He is described as King or Priest of Salem or King of Peace. Throughout scripture there is no one else who goes by the name of King of Righteousness, King of Peace, other than our Lord and Savior, Jesus Christ.

Therefore, tithing preceded the law and transcends the law as a practice to be applied today in the life of every believer. Later tithing became part of the law, Leviticus 27:30:

And all the tithe of the land, whether of the seed of the land or of the fruit of the tree, is the Lord's. It is holy to the Lord.

Further, we find Jesus reinforcing the practice of tithing throughout the New Testament, *"as something that ought to be done"* in Matthew 23:23. Thus, we see the fulfillment of the practice of tithing in Hebrews 6:20, Jesus is our High Priest after the order of Melchizedek. The priesthood of Christ is compared to the priesthood of Melchizedek, to whom Abraham gave his tithe. So often we want and claim the blessings of Abraham. If only we would desire the faith and obedience of Abraham as evidenced in his willingness to trust God and acknowledge Him as the Possessor of Heaven and Earth, the Most High God, the Resource and means behind all of his accomplishments. Tithing is a recognition of ownership. Abraham recognized that the victory he had just received, with only 318 servants, was not the result of their strength or great skill, but because God was with and for them. Tithing is a revelation of relationship. Your attitude toward money reveals your attitude about God.

Matthew 6:24:

No one can serve two masters; for either he will hate the one and love the other, or else he will be loyal to the one and despise the other. You cannot serve God and mammon.

Abraham's tithe to God's representative revealed his relationship with God as the possessor of heaven and earth. When you understand and truly experience a relationship with God, you can give God what belongs to Him without fear, speculation, or dread. If you know that your God is the possessor of heaven and earth, surely you won't fight to hold on to 10 percent, because He owns it all. In the book of Malachi, God says those who don't give the tithe are robbers. He doesn't call them thieves, or says you stole from me, but you have robbed me. A thief will steal from you and you don't even know they have — especially a good thief. However, the word rob suggests to do so openly, in your face – by violence or force, if necessary. When we don't pay the tithe, God says we are robbing Him in His face. To honor God with our wealth, is to live freely from the stronghold of financial stress and recognize that because your Father owns it all, 10 percent isn't worth stealing or hindering the release of God in your life. So, the next time the offering is taken in your church, remember He owns it all and has entrusted you with the responsibility to handle His affairs. So, give Him the honor He is due. If you want to truly gauge how much you really trust God, above your lip service, honor the Lord with the tithe!

The earth is the Lord's, and all its fullness, the world and those who dwell therein.

(Psalm 24:1)

Have you ever thought, sometimes I just can't afford to tithe? Do your finances reflect God as owner and you as manager, or would your checkbook or bank account reflect a lifestyle of self-indulgence vs. honoring God and His Kingdom agenda?

_____

_____

_____

_____

_____

_____

_____

_____

_____

_____

_____

_____

_____

_____

_____

_____

Closing prayer:

Father, forgive me for not honoring You as You desire with the wealth You have entrusted to me. Help me to realize that before I spend, I must acknowledge what belongs to You. I need Your guidance and wisdom to manage the wealth I have. Help me to be a good steward for Your glory and honor! Amen.

*Give, and it will be given to you: good measure,
pressed down shaken together, and running over
will be put into your bosom. For with the same
measure that you use, it will be measured back to
you.*

(Luke 6:38)

CHAPTER FOUR

First Seek to Be Givers

First Things First. In the last chapter, we discussed
the importance of honoring the Lord with our wealth, the
tithe. However, apart from the tithe, which we recognize
belongs to the Lord, Scripture commands that we give
more than just our wealth. We are called to give ourselves
to God. He doesn't make us give ourselves to Him,
although He could, rather he instructs us to do the
presenting. Our bodies are His temple, His dwelling
place, and, thus, are to be instruments of worship that
bring glory and honor to Him. We are to present or give
our bodies as living, holy, acceptable sacrifices. Not as
bodies that have been defiled by the pursuits of sin, but as
an offering that reflects our allegiance to Him. There are
several aspects of giving we are invited to participate in.

We are called to give thanks.

*Enter into His gates with thanksgiving, And into
His courts with praise. Be thankful to Him, and
bless His name.*

(Psalm 100:4)

Are you a giver of "thanks"? Do you enter into His presence with thanksgiving, or do you have to be provoked or reminded of His goodness? We live in a time where the simplicity of words like "thank you" have lost relevance and value. I can remember when holding the door or elevator for someone would welcome the courtesy "thank you." The neglect of such courtesy seemingly has gone unnoticed. Unfortunately, many bring that "thankless" attitude into their house of worship. Instead of offering God the thanksgiving and praise He is deserving, we act as though He should be glad we showed up. We are called to be thankful. Yet the psalmist charges us not to wait until the music plays or is just right, not to wait until you get that certain feeling. We are commanded to enter with "thanksgiving" upon our lips, blessing His holy Name. Thankfulness changes the atmosphere. It releases hope and expectation. It reminds those among us that God remains to be faithful no matter what. The unthankful among us will hear our thankfulness, and breakthrough can occur in their lives when we choose to give thanks!

I will bless the Lord at all times; His praise shall continually be in my mouth.

(Psalm 34:1)

David gave thanks because God responded to his cry for help and deliverance. It's difficult to complain when our mouths are filled with blessing and praising God. Every new day God allows us is an opportunity to give thanks. Just in case you're wondering, what do I have to be thankful for? Let me help you...are you breathing? Well, what are you waiting for, "let everything that has breath praise the Lord." Thanksgiving reminds us, all that we are and shall ever hope to be, is because of God's goodness to us. May realizing how great God's love is toward you fill your heart with unceasing thankfulness!

Not only are we to seek to be givers of thanks, we are to give to one another, to those in need, to the Kingdom, our resources, time and talents. To seek to be a giver is to look for opportunities to freely sow into the Kingdom and the lives of others, as God has so lavishly given to us. Giving includes sowing seeds of our time, love and helping those in need. We live in a time where the common goal is to receive, to get What we want... When we want it... How we want it. This attitude of receiving first further perpetuates the selfish mentality of this world's system that suggests "you deserve it." Have you ever pondered what life would be like if you received what you truly deserved? You probably would not be reading this book right now. Scripture records in Luke 6:38, *"For with the same measure we use in giving, it will be measured back to us."* So often when we think about receiving, we lose sight of the measurement used in our own giving. Giving of yourself may require lending an ear to listen to someone, or visiting the hospital to encourage someone, when you would rather be at home, having someone encourage you. As we first seek to be givers, we will manifest Christ's love and care for others. Giving is a timeless principle that God continues to use throughout Scripture to establish His purposes in our lives, enabling us to be recipients of His good treasures. In 1 Kings 17:8-16, we encounter a story that illustrates the importance of first giving to another. A widow finds herself in a hopeless situation, one she believes will result in death. In her despairing plight, she is approached by the prophet Elijah with what seems to be a very untimely, inconvenient request. He asks this woman for some food to eat. Isn't it interesting, when we feel we have nothing to give or are down to our "last," someone will ask for our "last". Unfortunately, that "last" often blinds us from seeing the provision God is trying to get to us. Furthermore, our "last" is never enough to meet our needs. Although the prophet's request disturbed this widow, what good was her "last"? Her "last" couldn't help her in the present and wasn't enough for her future. What are you holding onto that God is requiring you to give up, to offer to Him or to another?

So often it seems unfair to be asked to sit and play with our children, serve in ministry, attend another meeting, lend a listening ear to a friend, or share the gospel with the lost, especially when we are tired and down to our last. After all, wouldn't it be better to do so when we have enough (time, strength, money, or whatever the need requires)? I have discovered through the years that God's need of us is very seldom convenient, very seldom does what He require fit into our "perfect" schedules. This widow of Zarephath is an example of how many run their lives. First, to our own needs, and when it's all about us, seldom do we seek to look beyond to the needs of others around us. Can you imagine her thoughts when the prophet asked her to "first" bake him a cake. Bake you a cake? If Elijah was in the spirit, He would have known that she and her son needed something to eat. What would she do? What would you do? Seek first the Kingdom of God or the Kingdom of Self? She could trust in that last meal and tend to her needs "first" and suffer the tragic plight of starvation, or she could seize a moment that would forever change the destiny of her life and the life of her child. If she first sought to give, as the prophet requested, and took her mind off her needs, she would unleash the provision of Jehovah Jireh, the God that's more than enough. She would enter a realm very few Christians travel. Instead of trusting in what she could see, she would embrace the substance of the unseen, releasing the supernatural, unending supply of our heavenly Father.

One point worth noting, her decision to put first things first in giving wouldn't only affect her life, but the life of her seed. So often in our short-sightedness, we seek the moment without considering the life-long impact upon the future of another generation. Praise God, this widow of Zarepheth didn't live for the moment. She gave to the prophet "first" and received what God was trying to give to her, not just a momentary need being met. She came to understand that "man cannot live by bread alone, but by every Word that proceeds out of the mouth of God." The bin of flour was not used up, nor did the jar of oil run dry, according to the Word of the Lord which He spoke by Elijah. Until we learn to first be givers, we will limit the provision of God that awaits us. There is a provision of grace awaiting us, a provision of strength, a provision of resources available for us to accomplish God's purposes in the earth. Why settle for the moment, holding onto what God wants us to release to receive His unlimited supply. If you expect to receive God's best, then God expects your best. Let giving not be something to be considered only when we feel like it, or have the time, or can see a way to give. Rather, let us first seek to be givers instead of receivers that we may unlock the limitless supply of God's abundance for our lives. A giver never has to fear poverty or not having enough for themselves, for God sees to it that the giver receives back in proportion to what he gives.

Give, and it will be given to you: good measure, pressed down shaken together, and running over will be put into your bosom. For with the same measure that you use, it will be measured back to you.

(Luke 6:38)

What have you decided in your heart you are unwilling to give? Is it more of your time? Your gifts? Have you put them on the shelf? Are you a giver of thanks or has your speech become corrupted by complaining, murmuring and grumbling? Decide today to first be a giver of thanks, yourself and your gifts.

_____

_____

_____

_____

_____

_____

_____

_____

_____

_____

_____

_____

_____

_____

_____

_____

Closing prayer:

Father, forgive me for holding so tightly to my time and gifts. Help me to give You my time and gifts that I may be used for Your glory. Let the words of my mouth and the meditation of my heart be acceptable in Your sight. May thankfulness and praise always be upon my lips. I live for Your glory!

Call to Me, and I will answer you, and show you
great and mighty things, which you do not know.
(Jeremiah 33:3)

CHAPTER FIVE

First Seek to Be People Who Pray

First Things First. Has it ever occurred to you that the God of the universe, the Creator of heaven and earth, wants to talk to you? He really does. Yet many Christians never experience the intimacy which God so desires, our communion. What is prayer? Simply put, prayer is having a conversation with God. Prayer is making the time to become better acquainted with God and His plans for your life. It would be very difficult to know someone you don't spend much time talking to. Prayer becomes a vehicle that enables us to experience spiritual growth and become familiar with the presence of God. God invites you to call upon Him, to inquire of Him.

Call to Me, and I will answer you, and show you
great and mighty things, which you do not know.
(Jeremiah 33:3)

He assures us He will answer us. The Father is inviting us to call to Him as we would cry out or speak out to address a friend, to get their attention. He encourages us to seek Him in prayer, to cry out to Him, to call out after Him.

Unfortunately, many are praying less and fretting more, praying less and fainting, praying less and quitting.

The invitation to pray is God's initiative towards us. God invites us to seek Him in prayer so He may enlighten and empower us with what we need to rest in Him and stand confident upon His Word. He says when we call upon Him, not only will He answer us, but He will show us some great and mighty things which we do not know. Some great and mighty things that will usher a breakthrough in your life and the lives of your loved ones. So often we wonder why situations and circumstances seem to linger in the lives of those dear to us or in our own lives. Many believers have made prayer a last resort instead of first.

Scripture commands us to pray without ceasing, to pray continually and always. Prayer connects us to the divine will of God for His people and their situations. *"Your Kingdom come. Your will be done."* Prayer becomes a power source that fortifies and enables you to stand strong when the storms of life blow.

When Jesus found his disciples sleeping instead of praying, His response was,

> *What! Could you not watch with Me one hour?*
> *Watch and pray, lest you enter into temptation.*
> (Matthew 26:40-41)

I have discovered that many see prayer as a last resort because they have yet to make the connection that God, who is not seen, really does listen and care. It's actually more difficult to get those who you can see to listen attentively to what you have to say. Therefore, we often transfer the dynamics of our human relationships to our spiritual relationship. We assume God is like many people in our lives who may not listen or care about us. Thus we fail to see the value of first seeking God in prayer.

How does one break the cycle and make prayer a priority in life? How do I move past the barriers of endless silence? Where do I begin?

> *Be anxious for nothing, but in everything by prayer and supplication, with thanksgiving, let your requests be made known to God; and the peace of God, which surpasses all understanding, will guard your hearts and minds through Christ Jesus.*

> (Philippians 4:6-8)

First, *we must lay aside all anxiety.* Whether it's anxiety about how to pray, what to say, where to start, or anxiety about your circumstances, we must make a decision to cast our burdens upon the Lord, for He cares for us. As we prepare to first seek God in prayer, keep in mind God invites us to pray, which means He is more than able to handle what might seem burdensome to us. After talking to others about the issues we should be talking to God about, we are often still left in search of answers. Second, *talk to Him.* Use your own language, don't try to sound like someone else, just talk to Him as you would a friend. This is how you begin the act of prayer. Honestly talk to God and present the concerns of your heart. God welcomes us to be specific: "let your requests...". We should present all our requests to God, all our cares and concerns. God is the only one who can sufficiently handle our requests. He encourages us not to shy away from telling Him about the things that disappoint or trouble you. It delights Him that His children would recognize and look to Him as their only source. Third, *begin to thank Him.* Now that is a real step of faith. Many ask why should I thank Him for something that I don't see the answers to yet? Thanking Him acknowledges that God is able. You are to thank Him for several reasons: (1) that He heard you; (2) that He is able to handle it; and (3) that you already have the victory.

Now this is the confidence that we have in Him, that, if we ask anything according to His will, He hears us. And if we know that He hears us, whatever we ask, we know that we have the petitions that we have asked of Him.

(1 John 5:14-15)

Finally, as we rest in the assurance that God has heard us, we must embrace God's peace and allow our hearts and minds to expect God to show us the great and mighty things we do not know as we anticipate His answers and victory. Prayer will keep you from going your own way and doing your own thing.

There is a way that seems right to a man or woman, but its end is the way of death.

(Proverbs 14:12)

If you want to grow closer to your heavenly Father or learn to hear His voice and please Him with your life, *First Things First*...pray, talk to Him, become acquainted with Him and His ways, look to Him. Try talking to God first before running to others first. He is waiting to hear your voice, and He has something marvelous to reveal to you!

Trust in the Lord with all your heart, And lean not on your own understanding; In all your ways acknowledge Him, And He shall direct your paths.

(Proverbs 3:5)

Call to Me, and I will answer you, and show you
great and mighty things, which you do not know.
(Jeremiah 33:3)

What things have been hindering your privilege of
calling upon God and seeking His face? Do you need
assurance that God has heard you? Has prayer become a
first or last resort? Ask Him to show you ways you need
to return to Him in prayer.

_____

_____

_____

_____

_____

_____

_____

_____

_____

_____

_____

_____

_____

_____

_____

_____

Closing prayer:

Dear Father, please forgive me for forfeiting my privilege of prayer. Help me to depend on others less and more on You. Thank You for the assurance that You hear me when I pray and that You will answer my prayers. I desire a prayer relationship that allows me to approach You with boldness that I may receive Your direction for my life. Amen!

And be kind to one another, tenderhearted, forgiving one another, even as God in Christ forgave you.

(Ephesians 4:32)

CHAPTER SIX

First Seek to Forgive

First Things First. It matters to God how we handle our relationships. Do they reflect His love, longsuffering, and kindness? Our churches are filled with hurt and wounded individuals who have yet to forgive the wrongs of those who have hurt them. So often we think if we just pretend they don't exist or we don't see them, or stay to one side of the church, the pain and sin of our unforgiveness will disappear. Unforgiveness is a major stumbling block in the life of many believers as they seek to move forward to grow and prosper in their faith. They can only get so far without stumbling over this area of unforgiveness. Many have actually come to believe that it doesn't matter how we treat one another, as long as we are "right with God". Unfortunately, we fail to recognize the deception of being "right with God and not one another." We can never be "right with God" while harboring unforgiveness and bitterness toward those who also matter to the heart of God and are a part of His family.

Therefore if you bring your gift to the altar, and there remember that your brother has something against you, leave your gift there before the altar,

and go your way. First be reconciled to your brother and then come and offer your gift.
(Matthew 5:23-24)

Understand the priority God places on forgiveness. First thing, "leave your gift" and be reconciled to your brother, and then come back and offer your gift to God. So often we think we can impress God with our outward acts of service and loyalty while violating the first things. This verse makes it clear our gifts are not acceptable where unforgiveness fills the heart.

Then Peter came to Him and said, 'Lord, how often shall my brother sin against me, and I forgive him? Up to seven times?' Jesus said to him, 'I do not say to you, up to seven times, but up to seventy times seven.'
(Matthew 18:21-22)

Forgiveness is a principle, if you haven't discovered yet, that will be practiced again and again in this journey. Jesus had to remind Peter, *"I do not say, up to seven times, but up to seventy times seven,"* suggesting no limit can be placed on the number of times we must forgive others. Just when you think, "I can't take it," "I don't want to see or speak to them again," or "they will never hurt me again," you soon realize you're hurting yourself more than the other person.

Somehow when we refuse to forgive, that individual becomes more joined to us in a very unusual way. The harder we try to avoid them, the more occupied we are with them. They show up in our thoughts, our dreams, and our conversations with others. Have you ever thought, for someone I don't like that much, they are always with me? Instead of victory, we experience bondage as a result of the sin of unforgiveness. Thus, our life has become entangled with the offender. I am often asked how do I forgive someone who really hurt me? Many have attempted to walk in forgiveness, but cannot seem to reconcile or release the bad memories of the experience. First, we must understand that forgiveness isn't easy nor does it come naturally. The natural course is to retaliate and desire to see someone suffer to the degree we have. Although it is not natural, it is a necessary first thing in our walk with God that is possible by His grace and power. If you can imagine for a moment the decision for God to forgive us began with a choice, not because we deserved it, or were such good people in pursuit of His will for our lives.

> *But God demonstrates His own love toward us, in that while we were yet sinners, Christ died for us.*
> (Romans 5:8)

Jesus died for us and had compassion on us. He didn't wait for us to change, to become more loving or more deserving. Christ, being our example, models for us that forgiveness is a choice.

It must be a decision of our will as we seek to honor and please Him.

I don't think there will ever be a time, when we will feel like forgiving someone in this flesh. Yet the newness of life we now have hidden in Christ affords us the opportunity to move beyond what we feel and live by faith.

> *I have been crucified with Christ, it is no longer I who live, but Christ lives in me; and the life which I now live in the flesh I live by the faith in the Son of God, who loved me and gave Himself for me.*
> (Galatians 2:20)

Therefore, by faith we must first remind ourselves that WE no longer live, that WE died a long time ago, and the life WE now live is to please Christ. When we can truly grasp the principle of what I call the exchanged life, we will see that unforgiveness is not an option in the Kingdom of God. I can hear someone saying, "But isn't that a process? No one just starts off willing to forgive. After all, that forgiveness stuff was easy for Jesus, He's the Son of God." Yes, it is a process, a process that we must choose to practice immediately if we ever expect to walk in victory. Since the fullness of Christ indwells us, we possess everything we need, right now through Christ to live a life that pleases Him in godliness.

I realize, through counseling many, there are real hurts and pain that we all will deal with in this life. Things have occurred that we didn't ask for and probably didn't deserve. However, the adversary would love nothing more than to see people, that Christ has redeemed and set free, remain in bondage and captive to the ways of their flesh by allowing a spirit of unforgiveness to hold them captive. As we choose to forgive those who have wounded us, we are releasing the offender into the hands of a loving God, who can do a much better job at turning their hearts than we ever could attempt in our efforts of the flesh. Our failure to forgive others is directly related to our inability to receive forgiveness.

> *For if you forgive men their trespasses, your heavenly Father will also forgive you.*
>
> *But if you do not forgive men their trespasses, neither will your Father forgive your trespasses.*
> (Matthew 5:14-15)

Unforgiveness imprisons, it holds captive spiritually, mentally and emotionally. So often we think the only one imprisoned is the person who has wronged us or owes the debt, but we become the prisoners. For each attempt we make to move forward, we are bound by the matter we have yet to release. Unforgiveness holds a person to an act they can no longer change, the wrong has occurred and the kindest of deeds on their part could never replace their wrong against you. Why should we hold unforgiveness toward another? When all we have to do is "ask" Him for forgiveness, and He is willing and able to forgive us and remove our transgression so far from us. Maybe you have been trying to move forward and accomplish mighty things for God and can't seem to stay on course, can't seem to lay hold of the joy of your salvation.

First Things First, pause to see if you have taken anyone captive by the sin of unforgiveness. Chances are, if you have, you yourself have become a prisoner. *First Things First*, use the key of forgiveness and release the person(s) that you have allowed to hinder you from being all that God has called you to be. Forgive that you may free yourself to a lifestyle of victory in Christ Jesus. How can we be forgiven, except we forgive? There will never be a day when you and I will not need the forgiveness of God. Let us practice forgiveness that we may be forgiven. *First Things First*, make a decision today to forgive.

*And be kind to one another, tenderhearted,
forgiving one another, even as God in Christ
forgave you.*

(Ephesians 4:32)

Have you taken someone captive in your heart through unforgiveness? If so, say a prayer to release that person. Choose to let them go and tear up the files that keep them ever so close. You may want to write a letter addressing the pain, asking forgiveness and then shred it. There's a release in Christ awaiting you today!

_____

_____

_____

_____

_____

_____

_____

_____

_____

_____

_____

_____

_____

_____

_____

Closing prayer:

Father, thank You for forgiving me and not holding my sins against me. I admit I haven't been a good model of Your forgiveness. Forgive me. I choose to forgive (*fill in the blank*) _____. Restore to me a clean heart and allow Your love to flow through me towards them. May Christ rule and reign in my heart. Amen!

No good thing will He withhold from those who walk uprightly.

(Psalm 84:11)

CHAPTER SEVEN

First Seek to Walk Uprightly

First Things First. Could you tell someone, "Follow me as I follow Christ?" Or would they have great difficulty following the path you walk? Would the path you walk lead someone to the blessed life, or would they end up on a dead-end street? The word "upright" is to walk in a straight path. It signifies a course of conduct by which one leaves a straight track for others to follow. Why do we need to first walk upright? As believers, we are called to live in such a manner *"...that men may see your good works and glorify your Father in heaven."* Matthew 5:16. Our lives are to be infectious to those around us, causing those whose paths are crooked or headed on a destructive course to gain direction from our lives. Our lives should point to righteousness, as our lives light and lead the way to hope.

See then that you walk circumspectly, not as fools but as wise, redeeming the time, because the days are evil.

(Ephesians 5:15-16)

A decision to walk upright begins with our core values and our convictions. That aspect of our character that is constant and doesn't sway depending on the convictions or lack thereof of others. Walking uprightly begins with what's going on inside. The religious leaders prided themselves for doing all the politically correct things. They didn't touch this or eat that, resulting in a false sense of righteousness. Much like many believers today assuming that serving in ministry or giving money are signs of walking uprightly. Jesus reminds us where uprightness truly begins.

Woe to you, scribes and Pharisees, hypocrites! For you cleanse the outside of the cup and dish, but inside you are full of extortion and self-indulgence. Blind Pharisees, first cleanse the inside of the cup and dish, that the outside of them may be clean also.

(Matthew 23:25-26)

Today, it is easy to look upright, to sound upright from our external actions, and yet be far from God and the pursuit of His kingdom. We must come to terms that God isn't impressed with the outward, showy things we use to convince or impress others. Man looks at the outward, but God looks at our hearts. What good is it if we pray loud in public, and yet never pray in private? Or, if we demonstrate acts of service publicly, and yet are comfortable with lying, cheating, and living immorally when no one sees us. If we are to walk uprightly, we must invite Jesus to search our hearts. We, too, must examine our hearts to see if there is any resemblance of Christ. Are you seeking Him with all your heart, or seeking to be seen and pleasing before men? Uprightness begins with truth.

You desire truth in the inward parts, and in the hidden part. You will make me to know wisdom.

(Psalm 51:6)

God is concerned about how we walk.

Contrary to popular belief, it is not enough to simply confess Christ, but our lifestyle or profession thereof should point others to Christ. Uprightly speaks to our conduct, which leaves a straight track for others to follow. To walk uprightly is to travel the road less traveled. It isn't always popular to walk upright, to walk in truth, to speak the truth, to stand when everyone else is falling. Walking uprightly is to be willing to be a light when darkness seeks to prevail. To walk uprightly is to be willing to not laugh at that dirty joke, even though it's more popular to laugh just to fit in. To walk uprightly is to understand that a lie is still a lie, whether it's considered white, big or little. Jesus told His disciples in John 8:32, *"And you shall know the truth, and the truth shall make you free."* How can others know what is truth, unless we are willing to walk in truth, to stand for truth, to live for truth, and, if necessary, to die for truth? Walking uprightly is to be a man or woman of integrity, not when it is convenient or popular, but because it is RIGHT.

There is a wonderful promise in Psalm 84:11, *"No good thing will God withhold from them, who walk uprightly."* We have the assurance of everything necessary and beneficial for our lives when we live life to please our Father. Our church, marriages, children, and co-workers benefit from the good things when we dare to walk RIGHT. Not simply talk the talk, but talk and live for the glory of God!

> *And make straight paths for your feet, so that what is lame may not be dislocated, but rather be healed.*
>
> (Hebrews 12:13)

There are some lame amongst us who need healing, who need hope, who are desperately looking for answers. When we walk uprightly and walk straight, those lame in our path can look on and follow us. Those lame, broken, dislocated areas of their lives can be made whole as we declare "This is the WAY...walk in it, follow me as I follow Christ." Our walk should serve as encouragement to those who waver, and hope for those who limp as they struggle with areas of weakness in their life. *First Things First*, before we will see the manifestation of our heart's desires and prayers answered, we must make sure our walk is consistent with what God desires for us.

The Bible has a lot to say about how we walk.

Ephesians 4:1
Walk worthy of the calling with which you were called;

Ephesians 5:2, 8, & 11
Walk in love, as Christ also has loved us and given Himself for us..., Walk as children of light...and have no fellowship with the unfruitful works of darkness, but rather expose them.

May I challenge you? The next time you hear a sermon that really blessed you, don't just talk about how good it was. Allow the truth you hear to manifest in a changed life, walking uprightly that others can see and follow in the path of godliness. Let's first seek to walk uprightly and obey the words of God. John 14:21, *"If we love Him we will keep His commandments."*

Here are a few promises for a life that chooses to walk uprightly and chooses the path of righteousness.

Walking Uprightly releases the blessings of the Lord:
Blessed is the man who does not walk in the counsel of the wicked or stand in the way of sinners or sit in the seat of mockers.
(Psalm 1:1)

Walking Uprightly preserves life:
*Let integrity and uprightness preserve me, For
I wait for you.*
(Psalm 25:21)

Walking Uprightly manifests joy:
*Be glad in the Lord and rejoice, you righteous;
And shout for joy, all you upright in heart!*
(Psalm 32:11; Psalm 97:11)

Walking Uprightly brings peace:
*Mark the blameless man, and observe the
upright; For the future of that man is peace.*
(Psalm 37:37)

Walking Uprightly assures victory:
*Like sheep they are laid in the grave; Death
shall feed on them; The upright shall have
dominion over them in the morning.*
(Psalm 49:14)

Walking Uprightly brings deliverance:
*The righteousness of the upright will deliver
them.*
(Proverbs 11:6)

Walking Uprightly blesses the lives of others:
*By the blessing of the upright the city is
exalted...*
(Proverbs 11:11)

Walking Uprightly attracts the ear of God in prayer:
*The sacrifice of the wicked is an abomination
to the Lord, But the prayer of the upright is His
delight.*
(Proverbs 15:8)

Claim these for your life as you endeavor to walk
uprightly in every area of your life.

No good thing will He withhold from those who walk uprightly.

(Psalm 84:11)

Has your walk had a slight curve in it? Maybe on your job, in your speech, with your finances? What about your attitude? Instead of walking uprightly, you have turned a little to the right or left. Can others look at those areas of your life and walk straight as they see modeled by you?

_____

_____

_____

_____

_____

_____

_____

_____

———————————————————————

———————————————————————

———————————————————————

———————————————————————

———————————————————————

———————————————————————

———————————————————————

———————————————————————

Closing prayer:

Dear Heavenly Father, I invite You to search me, see if there is any crooked way within me. You desire truth in my inward parts. Not just truth when others are looking at me, but truth at the core of who I am in Christ. Take my life and use it for Your glory that others may see You in me and therefore follow the Christ I manifest, as I walk uprightly before You. In Jesus' Name. Amen!

This Book of the Law shall not depart from your mouth, but you shall meditate on it day and night...

(Joshua 1:8)

CHAPTER EIGHT

First Seek to Be Students of the Word

First Things First. How shall we live if we don't know His Word?

Man shall not live by bread alone, but by every word that proceeds out of the mouth of God.

(Matthew 4:4)

Are you living life by the Word of God, or by the words of men? Are you seeking to find out what others have to say about your situation, or is your priority to know what God's Word has to say about the matter? God's Word is our manual for life. Paul's word to Timothy, in 2 Timothy 2:15, instructs us,

Be diligent to present yourself approved to God, a worker who does not need to be ashamed, rightly dividing the word of truth.

When it comes to being a student of God's Word, it doesn't matter how many classes we take or how many sermons we hear (all of which are beneficial). Becoming a student of the Word requires first-hand exposure to God's Word for yourself. Paul told Timothy that diligence was something he was responsible for. Simply hearing about someone else's diligence to the Word doesn't transfer diligence to you. You must become a worker of the Word, one who can rightly and accurately handle the Word of truth. Unfortunately, we live in a time where it is more convenient to hear the Word than to study the Word. Maturity is not the result of hearing or receiving information about God's Word from someone else; we must know it for ourselves.

Yet many Christians live beneath their potential because instead of reading the owner's manual for themselves, they are content to rely on second-hand information. The problem with second-hand information is it flows out of someone else's understanding and experience, and, sometimes, interpretation. Second-hand information produces weak, malnourished believers who never fully grow up in the full knowledge of who Christ is. Why settle for crumbs when God wants to give you your own loaf. Why settle for someone's interpretation and understanding when your heavenly Father desires to reveal to you the riches of His kingdom found in His Word? So often believers are in pursuit of a Word from the Lord. This pursuit often finds them at one conference after another, in search of a special personal word from God. The tragedy of such pursuit is that dependency on words from others, instead of discovering God's written plan, rarely results in a changed life.

To become a student of the Word, we must start with our appetite. So often wrong food or junk food diminishes our appetite for the right food that is healthy for us. You must ask yourself what types of things fill my spiritual appetite above God's Word? What have you put in place of His Word in your life? Some replace God's Word with telephone time, television time, people time, work, family, or friend time. Whenever I ask the question, "Why is it difficult to become a student of the Word of God?" the common response is, "I don't have time." After listening to all the other things that have replaced their appetite for God's Word, I often conclude it is not for lack of time, but the inability and desire to make time. When I sit down to counsel individuals, I marvel at their responses as I point them to what God's Word has to say about their situation. Somehow the lights come on or there appears to be an understanding of the problem as they listen to me read and instruct them in what God says about their situation, instruction that they never knew was there. Absence from God's Word causes spiritual malnutrition.

So to become a student of the Word, begins with making a decision to see your spiritual appetite as important as your natural appetite for food. Refuse to allow anything to distract you from your spiritual meal.

> *As newborn babes, desire the pure milk of the*
> *word, that you may grow thereby.*
>
> (1 Peter 2:2)

In addition to having an appetite for the Word of God, you must desire the Word. There must be an intense yearning and longing for God's Word just as an infant desires and craves for milk from its mother. Having tasted the milk, the infant's desire grows stronger for that which is good and beneficial. As a matter of fact, some infants can't get enough of milk, they often find themselves desiring it so greatly that they take in more than is needed at the time. What that infant doesn't realize is that the more it craves and desires the milk, the stronger and healthier it becomes. As a result of such desire, we notice something, the infant begins to grow and keeps on growing. How wonderful it would be if believers found themselves not getting enough of God's Word, much like that infant, and desiring more and more. You may say, I know I should be a student of God's Word, but sometimes I just don't feel like reading the Word of God, I just don't have a desire for the Word like I do for some other things. How can I get a desire for God's Word? *"Oh, taste and see that the Lord is good...."* Psalm 34:8. I would suggest in order to acquire a desire, you need to taste again for yourself. Make a quality decision to open the Word of God and taste of God's special promises for your life, taste of His plans for your life, taste of His strength for your weakness.

Much like that infant who never knew milk (plain, bland milk) could be so good, it all began with a taste. At first you may want to spit it out by closing your Bible. Don't close your Bible, take another taste, read another verse, and another, and another. What are you doing? You are training your appetite to desire that which is good for you. The more you taste, the more you read it for yourself, your eyes will be enlightened to the wonderful things God has to say to you. You will discover how God has real answers to your real problems. This discovery will cause that desire to become even greater, and you will discover the beauty of a wonderful, growing relationship with a God who has much to say and show you about your life. Desire will soon turn to delight. In other words, you won't simply desire the Word just because you're spiritually hungry. The word "delight" means to be pleased with, to like, to will to do, something that provides pleasure, a source of happiness and joy. His Word will become a delight to you. You will discover His Word is the source of your joy, your peace, the source of your spiritual existence.

> *But his delight is in the law of the Lord, And in*
> *His law he meditates day and night.*
>
> (Psalm 1:2)

Desire becomes delight, whereby you won't just read the Word at special times, during specific situations, but there will be a delight to return to it all the time.

In addition to having an appetite, desire, and delight for His Word, becoming a student of God's Word requires being intentional. To be intentional is to make a decision to study God's Word on purpose, regardless of how you feel. Becoming a diligent student involves a commitment to work hard, to exert oneself, to give oneself to God's Word. In doing so, you are recognizing that God's Word has something that you need, and you are not willing to let it go until you receive all that His Word has to offer for the fulfillment of your life's purpose and plan. Becoming a student of God's Word leads to a prosperous life.

But his delight is in the law of the Lord, and in His law he meditates day and night. He shall be like a tree, planted by the rivers of water, that brings forth its fruit in its season, whose leaf also shall not wither; and whatever he does shall prosper.

(Psalm 1:2-3)

How would you like to see prosperity in your career, your marriage, with your children, in your finances, in every area of your life? It begins with a decision to become a student of God's Word.

The law of the Lord is perfect... More to be desired are they than gold, Yea, than much fine gold; Sweeter also than honeycomb. Moreover by them Your servant is warned, and in keeping them there is great reward.

(Psalm 19:10-11)

Prayer enables us to talk to God, and His Word enables Him to talk to us! *First Things First*, become a student of God's Word, make His Word a priority above all else.

Your word is a lamp to my feet, and a light to my path.

(Psalm 119:105)

This Book of the Law shall not depart from your mouth, but you shall meditate in it day and night.

(Joshua 1:8)

Can it be said of you that His words are more desired than gold and sweeter to you than honeycomb? Make a fresh start to put God's Word above everything else in your life. Examine your spiritual appetite and desires and get rid of those things that ruin your appetite for God's Word.

_____

_____

_____

_____

_____

_____

_____

_____

_____

_____

_____

_____

_____

_____

_____

_____

Closing prayer:

Father, forgive me for not giving Your Word priority in my life. Give me a fresh desire and delight for Your Word. Make Your Words sweet and desirable to me, even more desirable than things and people. I recognize that I really can't live without Your Word. Open my eyes that I may behold wonderful things from Your Word. Amen!

For the Son of Man came to seek and save that which was lost.

(Matthew 18:11)

CHAPTER NINE

First Seek to Have a Heart for the Lost

First Things First, Seek to Have a Heart for the Lost. Have you ever lost something that was valuable to you? Valuable doesn't necessarily mean it cost a lot. Value also speaks of the importance or worth of an object or person. In Luke 15:1-10 we see the heart of Jesus revealed as Jesus shows concern and care for those deemed as outcasts and sinners. The religious leaders of the day thought it was unthinkable and socially improper to welcome a sinner, or eat with them. As Jesus begins this series of parables, He responds to the criticism of the Pharisees' religious objection of sinners. They failed to recognize that Jesus wasn't just hanging out with sinners because He had nothing else to do. Sinners drew near to Jesus to hear Him. When a sinner was in the company of Jesus, they were hearing truth, they were encountering the love of God.

To help the religious leaders understand a sinner's importance to the heart of God, Jesus explains that a sinner is likened to that which is lost. A sinner, unbeliever, or unsaved person has lost his way and is traveling a road whose end is destruction. Jesus begins to remind the Pharisees of His purpose. The reason He walked the earth in the first place was for the sinner.

Jesus answered and said to them "Those who are well have no need of a physician, but those who are sick. I have not come to call the righteous, but sinners, to repentance.

(Luke 5:27-32)

He further declares that His mission is *"to seek and to save them that are lost"* Luke 19:10. It's sad to say, the spirit of the Pharisees has crept into the Church as many have lost sight of this mission... the Lost. As I spent time reading this 15th chapter over and over, God reminded me it was for this purpose that Jesus died for me...for you. We were all once lost. It was this purpose that Jesus died for many in the church. They were lost, but have been found. Unfortunately, the found want to dwell among the found and talk about what's wrong with the lost, and how bad off they are, and how sad it is to see them that way. We have become comfortable in our personal relationship with Jesus, having Him all to ourselves, to meet our needs, heal our wounds, and fix our problems, while we close our eyes to the fact that the Lost are all around us. Those, who were once like us, who have lost their way are headed on a fast track to Hell! In this parable, Jesus likens sinners to:

1) *Lost sheep who need a shepherd*: Like Sheep wandering...trying something different, searching, failing to see danger/warning signs, turning off the directed course of life.

We all have wandered away like sheep — doing our own thing.

(Isaiah 53:6)

2) *Lost coins that had value and purpose*: One coin was worth a day's wage...<u>it could be all one had</u>. It had value. People, like lost coins, have value, but become lost

through making wrong choices, hanging with the wrong crowd, painful circumstances.

3) *Lost sons who need to be in fellowship with the Father*: Like the Son lost through his own willfulness. There are people who are lost because they are determined to do it their way, no matter what. Often, they have to learn the hard way.

HAVING A HEART LIKE HIS...

1) *We must Pursue the Lost.* In the first two parables, Jesus shows us the importance of Seeking the Lost.

> *What man of you, having a hundred sheep, if he loses one of them does not leave the 99 in the wilderness, and go after the one which is lost? Or what woman having ten silver coins, if she loses one coin, does not light a lamp, sweep the house, and search carefully?*

Both parables illustrate the same point, but with different examples.

PURSUE: To work at, as a profession, to follow {another} with the intent of overtaking and capturing. Have you ever lost something of value, importance, or significance? The same effort that goes into pursuing that which we've lost should be our heart toward the lost unbeliever, that lost co-worker, that lost family member, that lost neighbor, or stranger in sin. Imagine, being out with a child and thinking he or she is lost, you're so connected to that child that you feel it emotionally, mentally, and even physically in your pursuit to find that child; or what about if you lose money, your paycheck, your car keys? Many of us don't rest until we have "Pursued" that which was lost. To "Pursue the Lost" requires recognizing the lost person God has placed in your sphere of influence. Like that coin, that lost person is a person of value, significant and important to God. That lost person is the one that Jesus came to "seek and to save." We don't have to look far for the Lost, they are all around us in our spheres of influence.

People matter to the heart of God. With all their idiosyncrasies, personality differences, people matter to God. Jesus said, "leave the 99". We can't Pursue the Lost while fellowshipping with the rest of the flock. To Pursue means to go after. God shows us in the first two parables the importance of actively going after the Lost, if a person is lost, they need to be found. We must pursue and seek. God does the saving. Pursuing requires taking our focus off self and having God's perspective about what matters most to Him. He came to seek and to save the lost. Some believers have so separated themselves from the world that many unbelievers don't even want to be around them. Jesus said He was the Great Physician, He went to where the sick were. He ate with those who had serious issues. He ate with prostitutes, tax collectors, who were known for cheating others out of their money. We, too, must go after, not be afraid to eat with, or to welcome sinners. It's only in the parable of the prodigal where we see God waiting with open arms for the son to "come to His senses," after a deliberate, willful intent on his part to separate himself from the Father's plan and purposes. However, it was still an attitude of love that awaited his coming to his senses and coming back home.

HAVING A HEART LIKE HIS...

2) *We Must be Persistent.* Persist – to take and maintain a stand obstinately, to continue without halting despite difficulties or setbacks, to exist in spite of adversity. We must Persist "until". We must persist with

an expectancy. In both of these parables there was persistency with expectancy that what was lost would be found. Imagine if we would pursue and persist after one lost person until they were found. Persistency requires time, patience, energy, love, and care on our part. That can be a long time, until the lost are found. That means we don't have the right to give up on people. There are enough people giving up and quitting on one another. Persistence says, "I care, you matter." We must persist because some lost don't know they need to be found.

Why is persistency necessary? Some lost people offer excuses for not coming off the lost trail of life, it's all they've known, they're not sure if what God has to offer is better if they've never experienced it. The thing we persistently look for, we will find! Persistency requires enduring "until," even when they say no, even when they appear they are not interested. We must continue in love in spite of the opposition. The persistent widow kept knocking *"until"* the judge gave her the relief she needed Luke. 18:1-5.

HAVING A HEART LIKE HIS...

3) *We Must Be Passionate.* Passionate to see the Lost found. Passion – a strong enthusiastic liking for something, intensity of feeling, or reaction. This passion is evident in the joy demonstrated over one sinner and the capturing of the lost sheep. Jesus happily puts the sheep on His shoulders and goes home. Shoulders speak to strength. The Lost need the strength of the found to help carry them. Passion doesn't mind bearing the burden of another. There's no record of the Shepherd reprimanding the sheep for wandering, much like nothing was said about the sins of the lost son. Just the love and joy in seeing that which was lost found! Oh, if we could have a heart like His. How quick we are to remember, to speak of what God

doesn't mention. God doesn't care about the details, only that they would come home and enjoy His purpose for our lives. It's interesting, twice the prodigal son says about himself, "I am no longer worthy." Lost people know their struggles, the shameful things they've done, they don't need us focusing on them, reminding them of the problems. They need to come to Jesus because He died for their sins, and regardless of their past, present or future, He has a plan for their life. His passion is evident as others are invited to celebrate,

Be happy with me because I found my lost sheep. In the same way, I tell you there is more joy in heaven over one sinner who changes his heart and life, than over 99 just persons who don't need to repent.

In order to become Passionate to See the Lost Found, we must ask God to:

1) RESTORE: Restore our hearts with His passion and joy to see the lost found.

Restore to me the joy of Your salvation, And uphold me by Your generous Spirit. Then I will teach transgressors your ways, And sinners shall be converted to You.

(Psalms 51:12-13)

2) RENEW: Renew our commitment to be about the Father's business ("souls") — to seek and save the lost.

Why did you seek Me? Did you not know that I must be about My Father's business?

(Luke 2:49)

3) REVIVE: Revive our hearts to be moved with compassion.

Then Jesus went about all the cities and villages, teaching in their synagogues, preaching the gospel of the kingdom, and healing every sickness and every disease among the people, But when He saw the multitudes, He was moved with compassion for them, because they were weary and scattered, like sheep having no shepherd.

(Matthew 9:35-36)

To prepare for the harvest, to be instrumental in receiving the harvest, we must have A Heart Like His...*A Heart that Pursues the Lost... A Heart that is Persistent toward the Lost...A Heart that is Passionate to See the Lost Found.* We live in a world where many are lost and without hope and purpose in life. Unless someone tells them, they will die in their lost state, helpless without God. When's the last time you actually thought about the miracle of your own salvation? That God gave you a new identity in His Kingdom and a purpose and part to play in His Kingdom. Doesn't that make you sit and say WOW! When you think of the awesome goodness God has shown to you, that you are alive, and will never have to die in your sins, such a joy and overwhelming praise should exude your soul that you can't wait to share the good news with others!   Maybe you have yet to discover your purpose, let me help you discover one big part of your purpose.

All authority has been given to Me in heaven and on earth. Go therefore and make disciples of all the nations, baptizing them in the name of the Father and of the Son and of the Holy Spirit, teaching them to observe all things that I have commanded you, and lo, I am with you always, even to the end of the age.

(Matthew 28:18-20)

We have been chosen and commissioned to carry His message into those spheres of our everyday influence, our places of employment, our neighborhoods, our schools, wherever we may find ourselves. We are to seek those who have lost their way and tell our story that God's power may change their lives and usher them into the purposes they were created to live. Just as the Son of Man, Jesus, has come to save that which was lost, we are His hands, His mouth, His feet to declare to a lost generation that,

> *God so loved the world {them} that He gave His only begotten Son, that whoever believes in Him should not perish but have everlasting life.*
>
> (John 3:16)

For the Son of Man came to seek and save that which was lost.

(Matthew 18:11)

Are you willing to be a laborer in God's harvest? Do you need boldness to share the gospel with those in your sphere of influence? Have you lost your compassion for those ensnared by a lifestyle of sin? Make a decision today to look for those divine appointments to share the love of God!

_____

_____

_____

_____

_____

_____

_____

_____

_____

_____

_____

_____

_____

_____

_____

_____

_____

Closing prayer:

Lord send me! Make me a reaper of Your harvest. Lord, thank You for the power of the Gospel that makes me unashamed, that equips me and moves me to have compassion for the lost. Help me to see that people matter to You.

But who can find a faithful man?

(Proverbs 20:6)

CHAPTER TEN

First Seek to Be Faithful

First Things First. Seek to be Faithful. How shall we reap, if we become weary and faint? Faithfulness speaks to loyalty, steadfastness, and trustworthiness. To be faithful is to be reliable, full of faith, knowing that He who has promised is faithful and is a rewarder of those who diligently seek Him! Faithfulness describes God's ongoing relationship toward us and what our relationship should be to Him and one another.

> *Great is thy faithfulness, Morning by Morning, new mercies do I see, all I have needed, thy hand has provided.*
>
> (Lamentations 3:23)

IT TAKES FAITH TO BE FAITHFUL. WHAT IS FAITH?

Now Faith is the substance of things hoped for, the evidence of things not seen.

(Hebrews 11:1)

To be faithful means there may be times I won't feel like it, I may not see my desired outcome, the substance of what I've hoped for, but, because I believe God is able to do what I cannot, my faith in God's ability enables me to manifest faithfulness to the person or responsibility I have been entrusted with. Faith is not a feeling, but a decision to trust in and believe in the character of God.

We live in a time where faithfulness to anything or anyone has become a quality to be desired. The willingness to be faithful to anyone or anything has become lost, as many seek to look to their own interests. The mottos "we only live once" or "you can have your cake and eat it too" echo from the lips of many as they seek to justify their inability to endure tough times in their relationships or careers. Who needs to be faithful, when I can just change jobs or swap partners when I feel like it. Unfortunately, this lack of faithfulness has found its way into the church. Many in the body of Christ have sought to justify their unfaithfulness to God, to their relationships, ministry, career, churches, and the like. The difference between the church and the world regarding faithfulness is that the world doesn't seek to impress you with being faithful and has no problem telling you that. The church, on the other hand, in an attempt to appear spiritual, will use clichés such as, "the Lord told me to." The Lord told me to leave my spouse when we discovered how different our personalities were, or when one spouse realizes the marriage is bigger than their needs being met. There's the temptation to abandon the covenant by being unfaithful to God and one's spouse. The Lord told me to get another job when I didn't get the promotion I was hoping for. The Lord told me to leave this church, especially after I was confronted about my sinful behavior. The Lord told me our season of friendship is over, not to mention I was offended by what you said. We seek to use the Lord's name to justify our selfish will and rebellion against God and His Word.

There are many instances indicated in Scripture where individuals faced challenges and endured difficulties. Yet, we don't see God instructing us to leave, swap, quit, or throw in the towel.

Instead, we discover Him saying,

For you have need of endurance, so that after you have done the will of God, you may receive the promise.

(Hebrews 10:36)

Having done all STAND. And let us not grow weary while doing good, for in due season we shall reap if we do not lose heart.

(Galatians 6:9)

We need to be those that will be faithful in good times and bad, not fickled, easily moved, allowing ourselves to be uprooted from the stations God has placed us in because winds and storms blow. God is looking for people that can be counted on. People who don't quit when times are rough, who don't run, who don't allow situations to cause them to forsake His purposes for their life; those will be the individuals who will hear,

Well done, good and faithful servant; you have been faithful over a few things, I will make you ruler over many things. Enter into the joy of your Lord.

(Matthew 25:23)

God never promised us that this life would be void of difficulty. As a matter of fact, He tells us,

In this world you will have tribulation; but be of good cheer, I have overcome the world.

(John 16:33)

That word "tribulation" describes pressure, the idea of being squeezed on every side. Yet in the midst of our tribulation, pressure, and stress, we can remain faithful and be of good cheer because Jesus has overcome the world. He has overcome every point of pressure and stress that will seek to overtake us and He is with us always. Faithfulness isn't based on the response or actions of others. Rather, faithfulness is a quality of the spirit that demands we look to God for strength and endurance necessary to handle the issues of life. He has given us His Spirit. His Spirit and power enables us to stand in the face of life's difficulty and endure trials. We are more than conquerors through Christ Jesus! When everyone else is throwing in the towel, giving up, and fainting, there needs to be a remnant of people who are doing exploits in the name of their God. A people who outlast and weather the storms because the greater One resides on the inside of them. Pressure is a revealer of what we are really made of. So often, our inability to remain faithful reveals a lack of faith, and our pursuit to have it our way instead of God's way.

First seek to be faithful, that you may inherit all that God has for your life. His grace is sufficient for you and His strength is still available to work on your behalf in times of weakness. Before you give up on that job, that friendship, or career – Pray! Remember, Jesus faced the cross in faithfulness to the call of God upon His life, not because it was easy, but He desired to do the will of His Father. In doing so, He was supplied with everything necessary to fulfill His mission in the earth. Your faithfulness to stand and endure could be the very tool that unlocks God's mission in the life of another as they realize, if you can stand, so can they. You can do all things through Christ who strengthens you. Remember quitters never win!

> *Therefore do not cast away your confidence, which has great reward. For you have need of endurance, so that after you have done the will of God, you may receive the promise.*
>
> (Hebrews 10:35-36)

But who can find a faithful man?

(Proverbs 20:6)

What have you decided to give up on? In what area is God calling you to a deeper level of faithfulness and commitment? List areas you could use more endurance in. When the going gets tough, how do you respond?

_____

_____

_____

_____

_____

_____

_____

_____

_____

_____

_____

_____

_____

_____

_____

_____

Closing prayer:

Father, forgive me for thinking more of myself. Help me to realize that You are always there and never allow more to be put upon me than I can bear. I make a new commitment to remain steadfast, to endure in tough times and not quickly loosen my grip. I look to You for the grace and power to sustain me and enable me to be faithful. Amen!

Is God First in My Life?

1. Spending quality, quiet time in seeking God's face first is a priority to starting and ending my day.

2. I will seek to allow God's love to flow through me rather than seek my own way through retaliation or holding grudges.

3. I recognize that I am a steward of God's resources and that He is source. The tithe belongs to the Lord, and I freely give Him what belongs to Him.

4. I freely give my time, gifts, and resources for the building up of the Kingdom and seeing the lives of others changed.

5. I am anxious for nothing, but in everything will first turn to God in prayer and supplication, with thanksgiving.

6. I recognize because God's forgiveness is so great toward me I choose to forgive others and walk in God's love.

7. I can be counted on to do what I say. I am a man or woman of integrity.

8. I delight in God's Word and am a diligent student of the Word.

9. I have taken my commission seriously to share the gospel. I am not ashamed of the gospel, I believe its power to save.

10. I am willing to stand the test of time and remain faithful in trials.

ABOUT THE AUTHOR

Deborah Y. Evans is the President & Founder of Victorious Living Now Ministries, Inc., a ministry devoted to equipping and empowering women to pursue their dreams and to live victoriously, by conquering with the Word. Deborah serves as an Associate Pastor at Emmanuel Covenant Church in Hyattsville, Maryland, under the leadership of its Sr. Pastor, Timothy L. Seay. In addition she serves as Dean of the Emmanuel Bible Institute.

Deborah is a sought-out teacher and preacher of God's Word, empowering many to Conquer With the Word. Her radio broadcast, *"Conquering With the Word,"* airs in several states. She has a bachelors degree in Christian/Religion Education and is currently completing her Masters in Christian Counseling.

Deborah and her husband, Roger, have two children and they reside in Fort Washington, Maryland. If you would like to contact Deborah for speaking engagements or require more information about Victorious Living Now Ministries Inc., write or call her at:

Victorious Living Now Ministries Inc.
P.O. Box 44-2345
Fort Washington, Maryland 20749
301-419-8208
Email: Contact@victoriouslivingnow.org
Website: www.victoriouslivingnow.org

RECEIVE JESUS CHRIST AS LORD AND SAVIOR OF YOUR LIFE

The Bible says,

That if you confess with your mouth the Lord Jesus and believe in your heart that God raised Him from the dead, you will be saved. For with the heart one believes unto righteousness, and with the mouth confession is made unto salvation.

(Romans 10:9-10)

To receive Jesus Christ as your Lord and Savior, sincerely pray this prayer from your heart today.

Dear Jesus,

I believe that You died for me and that You rose again on the third day. I confess to You that I am a sinner and that I need Your love and forgiveness. Come into my life, forgive my sins, and give me eternal life. I confess You now as my Lord. Thank You, for my salvation and my new life with You! In Jesus' Name, Amen.

Write to us. Let us know of your new decision, and we will send you information to help you with your new life in Christ.

VICTORIOUS LIVING NOW MINISTRIES
Pastor Deborah Y. Evans
P.O. Box 44-2345
Fort Washington, MD 20749
Email: contact@victoriouslivingnow.org

ADDITIONAL RESOURCES

For teaching tapes and additional products of Deborah Y. Evans Ministries and Victorious Living Now Ministries Inc., visit our website:

www.victoriouslivingnow.org

Email: contact@victoriouslivingnow.org